NEW YORK

DIAMOND PUBLISHERS

*With heartfelt thanks to a special friend
and invaluable editor, Judy Bobrow,
designer, Lisa Hajnal, of Grigg Graphic Services, Inc.,
volunteer CEO Barbara Cochran
and all the friends and "tipsters" who helped
bring this book to life.*

*Also, a special thanks to the
NYC Convention & Visitors Bureau.*

Preface

For nearly 30 years, I have been
happily spending two to four days a month
in New York for business and pleasure, and
I am still discovering New York.

In *Going like Lynn — New York* (the second book in my series of liberating travel
primers for women), I share my discoveries of this constantly changing, infinitely
fascinating city. All that is needed is a pair
of comfortable walking shoes, a sense of
adventure, a dash of curiosity and the will-
ingness to experience all the diverse sights,
sounds, tastes and aromas that are New
York, a city of endless surprises!

Even a short walk in New York can
become an event. Here is such an event
I recently experienced enroute to Lincoln
Center to see the ballet. I was strolling up
Broadway between 62nd and 63rd Streets
passing the Harmony Atrium. I looked up
and noticed inside the atrium dozens of
people suspended from a 50-foot wall.
It turned out to be the home of the Extra-
vertical Climbing Club, a group of urban
mountain climbers, and a little coffee bar
for spectators. Walking in front of me was
an elegant young couple off to some posh
event. Three not-so-young rollerbladers

passed me, almost knocking down a lady with carrot orange hair walking her cat (on a leash, no less!). This is just one tiny morsel of New York that I look forward to sharing in *Going like Lynn — New York*. The rest is waiting for your own discovery!

Just remember, whatever I recommend today can be completely changed tomorrow as New York City is an ongoing "work in progress."

I am looking forward to hearing from my readers about their own New York discoveries and wishing every woman bon voyage and happy journeys.

Lynn Portnoy

Table of Contents

New York
has it all!

Why New York?

New York fits my definition of a female-friendly destination based on these simple premises:

New York Offers Many Choices and diverse activities to appeal to women of various tastes and interests (as long as they like urban centers).

New York is as Safe as Any City if you take the necessary, common sense precautions of any large city.

Women are Accepted and basically well received. New York women have achieved prominence in practically every field and New Yorkers generally are comfortable seeing women in groups, in pairs or alone everywhere.

For women who enjoy world-class culture, theater, sightseeing, shopping, dining or whatever, New York has it all — in multiples. If you cannot experience it, taste it, watch it or buy it in New York, the odds are it probably does not exist.

Next, New York was selected simply because it knocks my socks off! It is the most cosmopolitan, exciting and adrenaline-charging city in the Western Hemisphere. After 30 years of regularly visiting Manhattan, I still feel my heart

pounding and my metabolism rising to full
speed the minute the plane lands.
I literally rush to the taxi stand and I am
on high alert — like my dog getting ready
for an exciting romp in the park. If I could
wiggle my ears in anticipation, I would!

Another equally important reason for
selecting New York is the incredible
human and cultural diversity found there.
People come from every nook and cranny
of the planet, all contributing to this rich
mish-mash of a city. Just stroll down any
avenue and you will hear a babble of languages. The extraordinary international
population allows visitors to not only hear
and see but also taste, experience and
encounter multiple cultures. Within a few
blocks, you can travel without jet lag,
exhaustion, time changes, passports or lug-
gage from one end of the globe to the
other. Just cross Canal Street at Mott and
you have traveled from China to Italy. It is
an extreme sensory experience of sights,
sounds, smells and of course tastes. From
latte to green tea, from pasta to Dim Sum,
it is all delicious and worth tasting.

For me, New York represents what
America is all about — a fusion of cultures
that is unlike any place in the world. It is
part of our unique heritage. Wherever
your family originally hailed from, you
can discover part of your own history and

culture as you visit the various neighborhoods, museums and cultural centers.

The following pages are filled with
my New York favorites. Every New Yorker,
every tourist, every travel writer has his
or her own special places. Hopefully *Going
like Lynn — New York* will be the catalyst
for the discovery of your own New York
favorites.

How To's
for a Three-Day
to Four-Day
Trip to New York

Pre-Planning

How To's for Packing

Travel with One Bag –
Wardrobe for New York

Female Safety Tips

How To's for a Three-Day to Four-Day Trip to New York

PRE-PLANNING

For me every trip begins with my purse-size notebook. It is always with me. These are the basics of my notebook:

- ✔ Close family member's or friend's home and office phone, fax or e-mail numbers.

- ✔ Credit card numbers with bank names, expiration dates and phone numbers to call if lost or stolen. Also write them on a card and put the card in your make-up bag (see "Female Safety Tips").

- ✔ Local car service or friend's number who will be picking you up (if not driving yourself to the airport).

- ✔ If applicable, drug and eyeglass prescriptions along with your doctor's name and phone number.

- ✔ Confirmation number for airline tickets, hotel reservations and theater tickets.

Three to four months ahead, choose performances, events or exhibits you wish to see:

Here are a Few Resources for New York "Happenings"

New York Times Sunday newspaper: Arts & Leisure for performance, museum and gallery information; sports section for events; travel section for hotel discounts.

New Yorker or *New York Magazine*.

Articles in your local newspaper and travel, food and lifestyle magazines.

Travel guidebooks for New York (see "Other Resources").

The Internet.

Friends and relatives who share your interests.

Resources, continued...

New York Convention & Visitors Bureau, 810 Seventh Avenue, New York 10019, Tel: 800-NYCVisit or 212-397-8222, fax: 212-245-5943. They are an incredible source of free information for a great trip to New York. Request:

- Official NYC Guide (also has discounts for a few hotels, tours, food and shopping).

- A New York City map plus tour and hotel brochures (walking tours, boat and bus tours, etc., schedules).

- Museum Book (has some discounts for New York museums as well as museums in other cities).

- New York City shopping guides.

- American Express discount booklet.

If friends suggest the name of someone to look up, call before you go. If possible, arrange to meet in the city for breakfast, a drink or lunch, so if you do not click, you have not wasted valuable time traveling to the suburbs.

Decide on possible dates to travel three to four months ahead and start checking for the best airline, train and hotel prices. Ask your travel agent to alert you to any airline sales. Check the Internet and newspaper ads for discount tickets or special hotel packages.

After deciding on a date, ask your travel agent to make airline and hotel reservations. (Request two or three hotels that appeal to you or call the hotel yourself.) You also can call hotel consolidators. (*Beware, most of them are prepaid and non-refundable.*) One number is Hotel Connections 1-800-522-9991. Others are listed in Sunday's *New York Times* Travel Section. Be sure to inquire about hotel and airline cancellation policies.

After booking hotel and transportation, decide if there is a special performance or event you must see. If so, call ahead for tickets. You can charge them to your credit card for a small fee (under $5). *Tickets are non-refundable!*

New York is busiest in May and June and September through December. If you are planning on these months, book your hotel well in advance. (You can usually cancel up to 48 hours in advance.)

HOW TO'S FOR PACKING

The trick to packing in one bag actually begins with buying your clothes. Ideal travel clothes are seasonless coordinates that can be layered. The fabrics should be lightweight knits or wovens in wool blends, wool, silk, cotton or good synthetics that will hang out easily in the closet or in a steamy bathroom.

I use two to three solid colors that will work well together, i.e. black, beige and red; navy and khaki with white and red accents in tops and scarves. Subtle tweeds work well in jackets mixed with solid skirts or trousers. Forget the loud brash prints for clothing. Save them for scarves or resort clothes.

10

TRAVEL WITH ONE BAG –
WARDROBE FOR NEW YORK

Just as cities vary, appropriate clothing varies with each locale. For instance, never wear sneakers in Paris because you are a perfect prey for thieves. However, sneakers are perfectly acceptable in New York. Many businesswomen wear sneakers with their suits to walk to work and carry their pumps.

- Since New York is a walking city, comfortable shoes are essential. Plan on three pairs — even for a weekend — one on your feet (a comfortable walking shoe), a second pair with a low heel or flats that are also comfortable, and a pair of dressier shoes for dinner or theater. (Remember it is often difficult to find a taxi and you might have to walk more than a dozen blocks.)

- Three to four sets of underwear (including the set you are wearing).

- Travel wearing your heaviest outfit — a good suit jacket, coat or raincoat. Pack a second lighter-weight jacket or knit cardigan.

- Wear comfortable pants or skirt on the plane and pack two bottoms (skirts or pants), including a bottom that makes a suit with your jacket that you can dress up with jewelry or a scarf.

- Four shells or sweater tops — pack three, wear one for a total of four for three days; pack four for four days for a total of five.

- Take a simple dark dress or suit. (Theater, ballet, concerts and most restaurants are not dressy — good tailored sportswear or dressy casuals work fine.)

- Take appropriate costume jewelry — pearls or chiffon scarf to dress up your dress or suit for a performance or dinner at a fine restaurant. Don't forget a small flat dinner bag for evening. I prefer one with a long shoulder strap that I can wear bandoleer style. These are chic as well as safe.

- Cosmetics and toiletries — shop for samples or trial size toiletries whenever you are in the grocery or drug store. It is one-tenth as heavy to have two tiny toothpaste tubes, cold cream, etc. as packing your large economy size jars and tubes. Beside shoes and heavy jackets or sweaters, cosmetics are the next heaviest thing in most bags.

- Remember you are traveling to New York, the shopping mecca of the world. Leave room for a few small, wonderful purchases.

FEMALE SAFETY TIPS

The major concern of women travelers is safety and security. Here are some simple suggestions that will help:

- Stay at small hotels, preferably under 200 rooms.

- Use the same street smarts traveling that you use at home. ***Trust your instincts***. Do not apologize for feeling uncomfortable. (I have taken a taxi for just a few blocks when I didn't feel comfortable walking even in a very good neighborhood.)

- Do not carry more than $100 in cash.

- Be sure to wear a jacket or coat with pockets.

- Wear a small shoulder bag under your jacket or a fanny pack around your waist.

- Keep $10 in your pocket for taxis or snacks so you won't need to open your purse on the street.

- Be sure to keep a card with your credit card numbers, expiration dates and toll free numbers to call if lost or stolen, as well as your traveler check numbers in your make-up or lingerie bag. If your purse is stolen or lost, you will have a backup!

- If you wish to give something to street people, keep McDonald's $1 gift certificates (or certificates from any other national food chain) in your pocket.

- Never walk on a deserted city street after dark.

- Walk with purpose — like you know exactly where you are going.

- Be aware of what is going on around you, of your total surroundings.

- When leaving an evening performance, walk with the crowds until you can find a taxi, or arrange for a car service to pick you up after theater or supper.

- If you feel someone is watching or following you and there is no taxi, go into the first open bar, grocery store or restaurant and ask the manager to call or help you find a cab. Many New York grocery stores are open well past midnight.

14

- Do not wear flashy or expensive jewelry when walking alone or using public transportation. The same rule applies for fur and leather coats.

- Try not to look like an obvious tourist with a camera dangling around your neck. Unless you are really into photography, carry a small camera in your pocket or tote bag or buy picture post-cards. The pictures may be better and there is less for you to carry.

Try not to look like an obvious tourist

I love

small hotels!

My Favorite New York Hotels

CHOOSING A HOTEL

The hotels listed in this section are my personal favorites because of their convenient location, comfortable size and reasonable cost.

When you stay in a small hotel, you can avoid the crowds, long corridors and noisy gatherings associated with conventions and large meetings. They are safer because the staff is more alert and knows the clientele. Doors are often locked after 10 or 11 pm, allowing access only to guests. There is a higher level of personal service and the staff tends to be friendly and helpful.

Rates vary dramatically according to the season and current demand. When booking your reservation, be sure to ask if there is a special summer or weekend rate and if the price quoted includes taxes and breakfasts. (New York taxes are $13\frac{1}{4}$ percent plus a $2 to $4 per night occupancy fee.) Wherever you decide to stay, try to book well in advance, particularly during May and June, and September through December.

MIDTOWN FAVORITES

THE WYNDHAM, 42 West 58th Street between Fifth and Sixth Avenues, Phone: 212-753-3500, Fax: 212-754-5638, Rates: $125 – $175. Located just down the street from the Plaza Hotel, Fifth Avenue shopping and Central Park, the Wyndham is a great choice. The Museum of Modern Art, Lincoln Center and Broadway theaters are within walking distance. The expensive but excellent Manhattan Ocean Club restaurant is across the street. Although there are 200 rooms, the hotel has the feel of a small European hotel. There is no restaurant or bar but a neighborhood deli will deliver breakfast or snacks that the elevator operator or bellman will bring to your room, along with anything else you might need.

The rooms are individually decorated and vary in size and style, giving each a quirky charm. (Avoid the dreary, small rooms on the second floor.) The plumbing is old and erratic but the service, safety and convenience make up for the occasional rust you might find in the bath water.

THE CARNEGIE HOTEL, 229 West 58th Street between Broadway and Eighth Avenue, Phone: 212-245-4000, Fax: 212-245-6199. Rates: $159 to $300. Another West Side location, this is a small (20 rooms) totally updated hotel with modern kitchenettes in every room. A complimentary continental breakfast is served in the lobby. The hotel attracts many foreign visitors and has the feel of a European hotel. **Rooms are prepaid and there is a fee for cancellation.** Call for current rates and refund policy. To reserve, you must call Hotel Reservation Network-Discount Hotel Rates at 800-964-6835.

The Manhattan Club, 200 West 56th Street at Seventh Avenue, Phone: 212-489-8488 or 888-692-2121, Fax: 212-707-5140. Rates: $250 – $350. Try to get into this luxury accommodation before it is sold out as a time-share (a new concept in New York). You are one block from Carnegie Hall, about eight blocks from Lincoln Center, eight to ten blocks from the theater district and a few blocks from Fifth Avenue. There are junior and full suites, all with complete kitchenettes, marble baths, terry robes, ironing boards, etc. throughout. Each unit is selling for $17,000 and up for seven days per year. However, at this stage of development you may still be able to rent a suite for under $300

20

a night that would be $450 in a hotel.
Breakfast is served buffet style in the pent-
house clubhouse, as well as cocktails during
the late afternoon and evening, for a nomi-
nal cost. This is a great value if you are
sharing it with someone. When making
your reservation be sure to emphasize that
you want the Manhattan Club. The reservation desk is shared with the Park Central
Hotel, which is attached. This is a large
tour group hotel that you enter from
Seventh Avenue. The renovated rooms are
around $199 but nowhere in the luxury
category of the Manhattan Club.

**THE SHOREHAM HOTEL, 33 West 55th
Street off Fifth Avenue, Phone: 212-
247-6700 or 800-553-3347, Fax: 212-
765-9741. Rates: $275–$325 (including
breakfast).** Located in the middle of
Midtown New York, close to Fifth and
Madison avenues where shopping, galleries, museums and restaurants abound.
You are two short blocks to the entrance
of the Museum of Modern Art. (MoMA).
Two of the city's best French restaurants
are on the same street — La Caravelle
right next door and across the street is La
Cote Basque. The hotel is a member of
the Gotham Hospitality Group, a well-
respected boutique hotel group. The hotel
has recently been enlarged and redecorated
in a sleek contemporary style complete

21

with white cotton Belgium sheets. There is
a complimentary breakfast and afternoon
tea. (There are sometimes specials —
occasionally as low as $159 — so ask.)

EAST SIDE BARGAIN

**HABITAT HOTEL, 130 East 57th Street
at Lexington Avenue, Phone: 212-753-
8841 or 800-255-0482, Fax: 212-829-
9605. Rates: $90 and up.** The hotel
boasts 90 rooms and an outstanding location in the midst of 57th Street boutiques
and galleries and minutes from Madison
and Fifth avenues shopping. It is sparkling
clean with new tiny ultra-modern rooms,
most with shared baths. There is a newly
opened lounge for complimentary continental breakfast. Reserve early for a room
with a private bath. If you are claustropho-
bic and need a larger room, you can
request a double corner room with private
bath (about $130). There are also some
large queen-bed rooms with marble baths
for about $170.

WEST SIDE BARGAIN

**PARK SAVOY HOTEL, 158 West 58th
Street between Sixth and Seventh
Avenues, Phone: 212-245-5755,
Fax: 212-765-0668. Rates: $95–$145
(including taxes and breakfast).**
One of the best bargains in New York, this

location puts you one and one-half blocks from the Plaza and Fifth Avenue stores like Bergdorf Goodman, five blocks to MoMA, two blocks to Carnegie Hall and a brisk walk to the theater and Lincoln Center. Breakfast is served next door in the postage-stamp-size pizzeria. (There is a complimentary continental breakfast coupon in the NYC Visitors Guide.) The lobby is minute as are the compact but clean rooms (96) with lovely modern baths — some semi-private and some private. Be sure to specify your preference. There also are a few suites with kitchens for under $200.

EAST SIDE FAVORITES

FITZPATRICK MANHATTAN HOTEL, 687 Lexington Avenue between 56th and 57th Streets, Phone: 212-355-0100, Fax: 212-355-1371. Rates: $179 $325. An Irish-owned, full service hotel in the middle of New York with an understated European ambiance, the Fitzpatrick Manhattan has 92 rooms and is loaded with charm and practical amenities. The

23

overall feel is personal and comfortable with friendly Irish service and lovely flower arrangements — definitely female friendly. There is a small modest restaurant — Fitzers, room service and afternoon weekday tea. Guests can use the fitness club around the corner and, for a serious rate, a Cadillac car service for airport pickups and drop-offs. There are occasional specials for as low as $159, particularly in the summer.

HOTEL ELYSEE, 60 East 54th Street between Madison and Park Avenues, Phone: 212-753-1066, FAX: 212-980-9278. Rates: $295 and up. This is one of my favorite small New York hotels. Its 99 rooms have been refurbished so there are lovely bedrooms and good bathrooms. The famous old Monkey Bar with its great murals has been restored and is still a popular meeting place for New Yorkers as well as visitors. The hotel is run like a fine European inn. Continental breakfast is served in the parlor on the second floor. The staff is accommodating, to the point of once lending me $20 for cab fare. You are around the corner from Madison Avenue shopping and galleries and walking distance to museums and great restaurants. This is definitely a splurge but still half the price of fancy luxury hotels like the Four Seasons, and if you stay a few days, a lovely choice. Call and ask if there are any special rates and if breakfast is included.

LINCOLN CENTER LOCATION

THE MAYFLOWER HOTEL ON THE PARK, 15 Central Park West at 61st Street, Phone: 212-265-0060 or 800-223-4164, Fax: 212-265-5098. Rates: $149 and up. I have included this hotel despite its large size because of its location (three blocks to Lincoln Center), proximity to Central Park and good weekend rates. It is a great choice if you are planning to attend a Lincoln Center performance and it is only a 10-minute walk to Fifth and Madison avenues shops and galleries. An old hotel that was half-residential, it has been redone and caters to many visiting performers and music and dance aficionados, as well as many European tour groups. It has a pleasant bar restaurant, the Conservatory that serves complimentary hors d'oeuvres. The rooms vary in size as well as price. The front rooms overlook Central Park and the windows are double-glazed to alleviate street noise. Try for a high floor with spectacular park views. There are many promotions so be sure to ask for the best weekend rate.

AN UPTOWN CHOICE

WALES HOTEL, 1295 MADISON AVENUE AT 92ND STREET, PHONE: 212-876-6000 or 800-428-5252, FAX: 212-860-7000. Rates: $199 and up. This is a great location for visiting museums such as the Metropolitan Museum of Art, Guggenheim, Whitney, Cooper Hewitt, Jewish Museum, Museum of the City of New York, Museum of the Barrio and hundreds of galleries, boutiques and auction houses. Another member of the Gotham Hospitality Group, the Wales is a delightful small hotel with 86 individually appointed and very comfortable rooms. Part of its charm comes from the beautifully restored Victorian parlor where you can enjoy breakfast, tea or a wonderful Sunday evening free chamber concert — worth staying over Sunday night and returning home Monday morning. When you enter the parlor with its highly polished woods and potted plants, you will feel as though you are a character in a Jane Austin novel. *Again be sure to request special promotions* as they can be 30 percent less than the regular rates.

New York dining...
Use my suggestions
or discover your own.

New York Dining

I can't begin to list all the wonderful dining choices in New York. Here are a few personal suggestions. You can also check the "Resource List" for names of books that will give you a more complete list. Don't hesitate to just walk down a street, read the menu posted outside and peek in. If you like the menu and the ambiance, and there are other diners, try it. You can discover your own personal favorites.

PRICE RATING
(without alcoholic beverage or tip)

Inexpensive	$10–$15
Moderate	$16–$30
Expensive	$31–$40
Very Expensive	$41 Plus

I have suggested inexpensive to super expensive restaurants. If you are on a tight budget, but want to experience a variety of New York's best eateries without mortgaging your house, here is my suggestion. Try the super expensive restaurants for appetizers and cocktails (moderate cost) or a prix-fixe lunch (also moderate cost). Or, instead of supper, have high tea if available for under $30.

All Around the Town

MIDTOWN

MILOS ESTIATORIO, 125 West 55th Street between Sixth and Seventh Avenues, 212-245-7400. *Expensive*. This is a lovely Greek seafood restaurant down the street from City Center Theater and only a few short blocks from Carnegie Hall. It boasts a stunning, contemporary décor as well as fresh delicious fish. I love eating at the handsome bar in this always-crowded restaurant. The staff is friendly and provides excellent service.

LE COLONIAL, 149 East 57th Street between Lexington and Third Avenues, 212-752-0808. *Moderate*. A Vietnamese restaurant with décor right out of an old MGM movie. There is an upstairs lounge bar with overstuffed settees, potted greenery and tin ceilings with fans. It is located a half block from the Fitzpatrick Hotel and the Habitat Hotel.

TEODORA, 141 East 57th Street between Lexington and Third Avenues, 212-826-7101. *Moderate.* Small, wonderfully friendly staff and delicious uncomplicated Northern Italian cuisine make this a great Midtown find. (Because it was so good and so comfortable, I ate here two nights in a row after the theater.)

MARICHU, 342 East 46th Street between First and Second Avenues, 212-370-1866. *Moderate.* You can sample the Basque cuisine of Northern Spain for lunch or dinner in a charming, intimate setting near the United Nations. The food is wonderful with interesting subtle spices prepared by a female chef from Spain. Her husband runs the small dining room and summer terrace.

MANHATTAN OCEAN CLUB, 57 West 58th Street at Sixth Avenue, 212-371-7777. *Very Expensive.* One of the best restaurants in New York with fine wine and wonderful fresh fish and seafood superbly prepared. The atmosphere is beautiful with Picasso ceramics displayed on the walls. The service is extremely female friendly. The gracious maitre d' and good waitstaff make everyone feel welcome. One of my favorite splurges here is a late lunch of cold lobster salad and a glass of crisp dry French Chablis.

OSTERIA D'ANGELO, 242 West 56th Street between Broadway and Eighth Avenue, 212-307-0700. *Moderate.* This is a small local Italian restaurant with a pleasant staff and very good food for a decent price. It offers good value and location for Lincoln Center, City Center and Carnegie Hall and for a pleasant change — a New York restaurant quiet enough for conversation. I especially enjoy the grilled calamari (squid) served over salad.

LA CREPE DE BRETAGNE, 46 West 56th Street, 212-245-4565. *Moderate.* A wonderful spot for Sunday supper offering delicious well-presented bistro fare in a simple setting. (The French chef has worked at Maxims.) Try the mussels and pommes frites (French fries) as well as the fish selections.

TRATTORIA DELL'ARTE, 900 Seventh Avenue between 56th and 57th Streets, 212-245-9800. *Moderate.* One of my favorites, it offers good food, a large selection for vegetarians and calorie counters, and is very comfortable for single women. You will find the largest antipasti selection outside of Italy (vegetables or seafood cooked and served at room temperature). The antipasti bar is tiny with room for only about ten diners. If you are alone, it is more fun to sit here to select your meal than at a table. Also, the

31

servers and diners are all very congenial.
You can also order a full dinner from
the menu if you prefer. It is always busy
and if you want a table, call ahead for
reservations.

**KABUL CAFÉ, 265 West 54th Street
between Broadway and Eighth Avenue,
212-757-2037.** *Inexpensive.* An attractive
upstairs Afghani dining room offering a
dining adventure. There are kabobs
(grilled chicken or lamb) as well as many
vegetarian entrees. The food is delicious
(not spicy) and the staff is very friendly.
The kitchen is a little slow, so allow
extra time.

**PETROSSIAN, 182 West 58th Street
at Seventh Avenue, 212-245-2214.**
Expensive to Very Expensive. This is a
branch of Petrossian from Paris and
known throughout the world for its caviar
and paper-thin smoked salmon. It is fun
to come here before or after theater and
enjoy the luxury of a glass of champagne
or vodka, smoked salmon, caviar, blinis, a
green salad, and fresh raspberries or
strawberries instead of a full dinner in a
moderate restaurant. Or come for a prix
fixe lunch or dinner. (Inquire when reserv-
ing.) A very sophisticated atmosphere with
more European languages spoken at
neighboring tables than English.

CENTRAL MIDTOWN

BRYANT PARK GRILL AND CAFÉ, 25 West 40th Street, behind the main New York Library, 212-840-6500. *Moderate to Expensive.* The setting, overlooking Bryant Park greenery, is a fantastic oasis in the middle of Manhattan. This is a wonderful place for a late lunch either outside in the café or inside in the grill. The menu offers light main courses and lovely salads. For a perfect summer lunch, try a cold lobster salad with a glass of chilled dry white wine. (I love fresh lobster salad and it is not easy to find in suburban Detroit, where I live, so I happily splurge in New York.) While in the neighborhood, be sure to visit the beautifully restored New York Library. It is one of the jewels of New York.

NEAR LINCOLN CENTER

JOSEPHINA, 1900 Broadway between 63rd and 64th Streets, 212-799-1000. *Moderate.* Conveniently located across the street from Lincoln Center, the food is average but the people watching is often great! It is a good idea to come here for dessert after a performance, then find a taxi after the crowds have thinned.

CAFÉ DES ARTISTES, 1 West 67th Street between Columbus and Central Park West, 212-877-3500. *Expensive.* This is a super comfortable spot for women. (I often order two wonderful appetizers before a performance for the perfect early supper.) I love the cold asparagus and smoked salmon. Beautiful flowers and murals provide a great spot for people watching. Reservations are a must. You can dine at the bar if you wish. There is always a friendly and interesting group of regulars.

Great Midtown Bargain Restaurants

WEST SIDE

MAXIMILLIAN CAFÉ, 926 Seventh Avenue between 58th and 59th—a half block walk from Central Park, 212-333-5150. *Inexpensive.* A cute, tiny neighborhood café with fresh, delicious, simple food as well as imported Scotch salmon and Beluga caviar—a real find! You can have wonderful omelets, sandwiches, crepes, soups and salads, as well as four or five choices of hot entrees. I had a huge real (not processed) roasted white meat

of turkey sandwich on fresh rye bread for under $10. The sandwich could have easily been shared with a friend. The café is open Monday through Sunday, 8 am to 7 pm, for breakfast, lunch and dinner.

LE SOLEIL, 877 Tenth Avenue between 57th and 58th Streets, 212-581-6059. *Really Inexpensive.* The delicious Haitian food, primitive Haitian pictures decorating the walls and the lilting French Creole conversations offer a wonderful adventure. Three different Haitian cab drivers recommended this storefront Caribbean restaurant to me and I wasn't disappointed. For under $12 you can have your choice of three or four main courses like Lambi (conch), a fish, or usually a chicken dish with rice and beans. The clientele are mainly Caribbean males and everyone is very friendly and gracious.

THEATER DISTRICT

ORSO, 322 West 46th Street between Eighth and Ninth Avenues, 212-489-7212. *Moderate.* This small Italian restaurant has a friendly staff, good pasta, thin crusted pizzas and a nice selection of main courses. They are always busy so you'll need a reservation. Great Italian pottery from the Amalfi coast adds to the charm of the restaurant. It is very female comfortable.

TOUT VA BIEN, 311 West 51st Street, a few doors west of Eighth Avenue, 212-265-0190. *Moderate.* This French bistro is one of the oldest small restaurants in the district. The current owner is a wonderful host and makes all guests feel welcome. The original owners (Nina from Marseilles and husband, Carlo from Genoa) often visit and hold court at the tiny bar after 7:30 pm. Great old-time, efficient, no nonsense waitresses. Best pommes frites (French fries) in town, and on Friday they do a bouillabaisse at a reasonable price. I love the old-fashioned menu of filet of sole, mussels, calves liver and coq au vin. The food is great and the ambiance cheerful. It is hard to go wrong here and the bill is always a happy surprise — extremely reasonable for the quality.

36

DOWNTOWN–VILLAGE AND SOHO

GOTHAM BAR & GRILL, 12 East 12th Street between Fifth Avenue and University Place, 212-620-4020. *Expensive.* Offers beautiful and delicious cuisine. Great service and a lovely setting make this a perennial favorite. One of Zagat's top-rated restaurants. Come for a late lunch at a great price, $19.95, and enjoy without spending a fortune.

LA BOHEME, 24 Minetta Lane between Bleeker and West 3rd Street, 212-473-6447. *Inexpensive to Moderate.* This adorable inexpensive French bistro in Greenwich Village is right next to the Minetta Lane Theater. I enjoy the neighborhood ambience as well as the well-prepared food and wine. Try the mussels and pommes frites.

BAMBOU, 243 E. 14th Street between Second and Third Avenues, 212-358-0012. *Expensive.* This elegant Caribbean restaurant in the East Village is filled with a beautiful young Caribbean and American crowd. The fish tastes almost as fresh as it does in the Caribbean. Come for a lively evening with great people watching in a veritable tropical setting.

BALTHAZAR, 80 Spring Street, 212-965-1414. *Moderate.* A busy French bistro in SoHo with a wonderful Parisian bistro menu. You will feel as if you have been "zapped" to Paris. There is a chic young clientele and although it is difficult to get reservations, perfect for a late lunch when the crowd thins.

CHINATOWN

HUNG SUN NOODLE SHOP, 115 Mott Street, 212-965-9663. *Very Inexpensive.* There are only four Formica tables in this basically carryout Chinese noodle shop. The steamed buns start at 30 cents and are absolutely delicious. An order of eight steamed crabmeat buns is $5.50. This is an adventure costing what a meal was twenty or thirty years ago.

HARLEM

LONDELS, 2620 Frederick Douglass Blvd. bordered by West 139th and 140th Streets, 212-234-6114. *Moderate.* Go for a delicious "soul food" Sunday brunch buffet. The staff welcomes everyone like a regular — I loved it!

Three Very Special Restaurants

DOWNTOWN NEW YORK

CAPSOUTO FRERES, 451 Washington Street at the corner of Watts, 212-966-4900. *Moderate to Expensive.* Enjoy a wonderful dinner served in a romantic setting — a cleverly restored warehouse. *Do not miss* the "out of this world soufflés." They must be ordered at the same time as your main course. When you call for reservations, ask for exact directions from your hotel and give them to the taxi driver. It will cost about $10 to get there.

BOULEY BAKERY, 120 West Broadway between Duane and Rcade Streets, 212-964-2525, Bakery and Carryout— *Inexpensive.* **Dining Room —***Expensive to Very Expensive.* The food at this TriBeCa restaurant is so delicious and so beautifully presented by friendly servers and maitre d's that I think it is one of the best meals in New York. My recommendation — this is a splurge you owe yourself. I went recently for a late lunch with a few friends after visiting Ellis Island and before a stroll through the boutiques and galleries of SoHo. Every course was an incredible treat and the breads — the best in New York.

UPTOWN

PICHOLINE, 35 West 64th Street between Broadway and Central Park West, a few blocks from Lincoln Center, 212-724-8585. *Expensive to Very Expensive.* Call way ahead for reservations at this popular excellent restaurant. Chef Terrance Brennan prepares delectable cuisine served by a competent waitstaff. As terrific as the dinner is, wait until you see the cheese cart. There are over 100 cheeses accompanied by a real live cheese "sommelier."

Sometimes I go just for the cheese cart and a glass of wine. The price for the cheese is astronomical, but it is a gastronomic experience (even if you have to carry your lunch for a month). Ask for Daniel to be your waiter. He is also from Detroit and will make you feel welcome in this elegant restaurant.

A Few Places
for Lovely Afternoon Tea

PAYARD PATISSERIE & BISTRO, 1032 Lexington Avenue between 73rd and 74th, 212-717-5252. *Inexpensive to Moderate.* Tea is served from 3 to 5 pm The pastry chef, Francois Payard and Chef guru, Daniel Bolud, have joined forces to create the perfect Parisian patisserie. (Calorie counters — beware!)

THE LOBBY LOUNGE AT THE FOUR SEASONS, 57 E. 57th Street between Madison and Park Avenues, 212-758-5700. *Expensive.* Teatime is from 3 to 5 p m in the lobby of one of New York's most expensive chic hotels. Afternoon tea here will make you feel rich and pampered.

THE ASTOR COURT AT THE ST. REGIS, 2 E. 55th Street between Madison and Fifth Avenue, 212-753-4500. *Expensive.* Come from 3 to 5:30 pm for a three-course tea served with silver teapots. This is an elegant experience with Porthault linens (the French linens of royalty) and fine porcelain cups and saucers.

THE TEA BOX AT TAKASHIMAYA, Fifth Avenue between 54th and 55th Streets, 212-350-0100. *Inexpensive to Moderate.* Stop for a relaxed teatime any day but Sunday. Enjoy the quiet ambiance of this elegant Japanese department store.

THE PALM COURT AT THE PLAZA HOTEL, Fifth Avenue between 58th and 59th Streets, 212-759-3000. *Moderate to Expensive.* Daily tea is served where the fictional Eloise flourished. Teatime is still a hallowed tradition here. It is like being in the "50s" complete with harp and piano duets.

LADY MENDL'S TEA SALON AT THE INN AT IRVING PLACE, 56 Irving Place between 15th and 16th Streets, 212-533-4466. *Expensive.* A five course English tea is served Wednesday through Sunday in the salon of this charming Victorian townhouse. Lady Mendl's is a special treat — complete with smoked salmon tea sandwiches and homemade scones with clotted crème. You also can stay at this beautiful inn.

WILD LILY TEA ROOM IN CHELSEA, 511 W. 22nd Street, 212-691-2258. *Inexpensive to Moderate.* Just walk through the door and you will feel the amazing tranquility of this charming setting — a lovely neighborhood addition. Along with tea, there are classical music concerts on some afternoons. Call for the schedule. Even if you are visiting on a day without music, you will enjoy the tea and assorted sandwiches or dumplings. It is closed Mondays.

Great Bars for Viewing, Being Viewed and Light Meals

BAR AT THE RAINBOW GRILL AT 30 ROCKEFELLER PLAZA. (65th floor)
The view, night or day, overlooks the whole island of Manhattan. It is just plain spectacular. You can order a light snack here in lieu of lunch or supper for one-fifth the price on the restaurant side.

MONKEY BAR AT ELYSEE HOTEL, 60 E. 54th between Madison and Park.
Renovated New York landmark bar with original murals. Great people watching. Both local New Yorkers and international visitors gather here for a pre-dinner drink.

**THE BAR AT JEAN GEORGES RESTAU-
RANT IN THE TRUMP INTERNATIONAL
HOTEL, #1 Central park between 60th
and 61st Streets.** One of the newest
expensive hotels and restaurants in New
York, a few blocks from Lincoln Center.
I recently enjoyed a crab appetizer and
glass of wine at the contemporary bar
for under $20. Throughout the room are
exquisite flower arrangements by a highly
creative floral designer in SoHo, David
Brown of the *Flower Shop*.

The bars at the Four Seasons and St.
Regis that I mentioned for tea are equally wonderful for drinks and appetizers.
Also enjoy any of the new, small martini
and champagne bars springing up.

*For women dining alone: At regular bars,
(not restaurants with little waiting bars)
request a table and you will not be has-
sled. (Exception – the small bars in the
hotels recommended here are fine for
chatting with bartender or guests.)*

Tips for Women Dining Out

Sometimes, even if you are traveling with a companion, there is an evening where you have different plans. I have included suggestions for dining with a female companion as well as tips for dining alone that should help promote better service for women diners. Here are a few suggestions for feeling comfortable in a good restaurant:

- Call for reservations and say you appreciate good service and a pleasant table.

- Enter the restaurant with confidence. You are a well-dressed, attractive woman with a presence that says you belong, whether dining alone or with a companion.

- Do not be intimidated. Try picturing the maitre d' standing there naked. That image should bring you an instant chuckle and terrific smile. This vision will calm you and put you in a festive mood.

45

- When ordering dinner and several things sound interesting, ask your waitperson or maitre d' for suggestions.

- If alone, after your drink arrives (even if it is mineral water), take a few sips. Then take out your small pocket notebook and slowly write your first impressions of the restaurant, including what you ordered for dinner. Put your notebook back in your purse when your first course arrives and smile sweetly at the waiter and your neighbors at the next table. They will probably think you are a restaurant critic and are taking notes. You might find this little exercise at least brings you great service.

- A nonverbal diversion is to observe the other diners and try to figure out relationships, where and how they live, what they do, and a little private fantasy guessing game. Again, write your impressions in your notebook. (This could be the start of a new career!)

- If you have enjoyed your dinner and had good service, remember to tip at least 15 percent and up to 20 percent in a fancy restaurant.

- If you are alone, try dining at the small front bar that most upscale restaurants have for diners waiting for their table.

Call and ask if they will serve you dinner at the bar. Most restaurants will happily accommodate you.

Advantages of Restaurant Bars — Bars are generally friendlier with waiters, bartender and guests chatting together. You are already dining while others do not even have their table or a menu. People will be eager to find out what you are eating, making you an instant food guru.

Sushi or Antipasti Bar...Great Alone or with Companion — The sushi chefs or antipasti servers are knowledgeable about their respective cuisine and are trained to be sociable and explain their culinary delights. It's just plain fun! In New York, you can literally travel the world on your stomach and enjoy every tasty "morceau" (tiny bite).

Go! See! Do!

Where to Go and What to See

Sensory treasures await you around
every corner of New York. Take a horse
and buggy ride through Central Park; sit
in the lobby of the Plaza Hotel; shop the
department stores, galleries and fine
boutiques of the Upper East Side and
meander through the neighborhoods of
Greenwich Village, SoHo, Little Italy
and the lower East Side. Visit the United
Nations, Rockefeller Center, Grand Central
Station, the World Trade Center, Battery
Park, Ellis Island and the Statue of Liberty.
Go to the theater and visit the museums.
The list is endless, making it necessary to
return again and again to this magical city.

Here are a few off-the-beaten-path destinations not to be missed!

- Take tea at Lady Mendl's Tea Room (Wednesday–Sunday).

- Enjoy free tango dancing at Chelsea Market (Saturday 4–7 pm).

- View the Statue of Liberty framed by the public restroom structure in Robert Wagner Park.

- Shop for wonderful bargains at Kam Man Market in Chinatown.

- Take a free Big Apple Greeters walking tour or a bicycle tour from Central Park Bicycle Tours ($30 including bicycle).

- Visit the tiny Chinese gallery, Feng Shiu, on Eldridge Street and explore the food, spice, candy and bakery shops after touring the fascinating Lower East Side Tenement Museum and Eldridge Street Synagogue.

Off-the-beaten-path destinations continued...

- Walk through the rose garden (facing the East River outside the United Nations) after dining in the delegate's dining room.

- Visit Harlem, with brunch at Londels.

- Try one new exotic cuisine — Haitian, a Chinese Noodle Shop, Afghan, Japanese, Vietnamese, etc.

- Attend a free concert. You can listen to chamber music on Sunday evenings at the Wales Hotel. (Call 212-876-6000.) Or attend a summer American music concert on Friday or Saturday evening at MoMA in the sculpture garden. (Enter from 54th Street.)

- Attend a student performance of dance, theater or music at Fiorello LaGuardia High School for the Performing Arts at Lincoln Center. Tickets are $6. Call 212-496-0700.

- Take advantage of inexpensive performances or tours from the 92nd Street "Y." Call 212-415-5599.

EXPERIENCE NEW YORK'S PARKS, GARDENS AND VIEWS

The Conservancy at Central Park, Rockefeller Center's Channel Gardens, pocket parks all around Midtown.

The view of the Hudson River from Riverside Park (West Side). Spring through fall enjoy it from the Boat Basin Café. Enter on West 79th Street.

Spectacular views of Manhattan from Windows of the World — on top of the World Trade Center, the Rainbow Room at Rockefeller Center, the top deck of the Intrepid Air Carrier, the walk along the waterfront at Battery and Robert Wagner Parks.

Views from the water: The Staten Island Ferry, the Ellis Island and Statue of Liberty Ferries or any of the tour cruises.

View of Central Park from the roof Sculpture Garden of the Metropolitan Museum of Art.

HOW TO GO AND SEE

By foot, bus, sightseeing bus, Big Apple Hop-on Hop-Off bus, tour boat or ferry, pedicab, horse-drawn carriage, taxi or private car service. It's your choice! (*I omitted the subway because you miss the sights along the way.*)

Whatever your interest...

New York has a museum.

My Favorite Museums

New York has dozens of fascinating museums. Choose those that appeal to your particular interests. Remember to check the *New York Times* for listings of current exhibitions.

**THE MUSEUM OF MODERN ART (MoMA),
11 West 53rd Street, 212-708-9480.
Hours: Saturday through Tuesday –
11 am to 6 pm; Thursday and
Friday – Noon to 8 pm; closed
Wednesday.** MoMA is like "puppy heaven" for anyone interested in late 19th and 20th Century art. Do not miss the sculpture garden. It is fun to relax here and sip a cold drink in the summer while you contemplate a Picasso or Maillol or whatever sculpture catches your fancy. There are free summer concerts on Friday and Saturday evenings outdoors in the sculpture garden. Either get there an hour early to find a place or make reservations on the

terrace above it at Sette Moma for dinner (212-708-9710). The dinner is just adequate but the setting and free concert compensate. A lovely way to spend a summer evening—listening to contemporary music performed by students of the Juilliard School of Music.

METROPOLITAN MUSEUM OF ART (Met), Fifth Avenue at 82nd Street, 212-535-7710. Hours: Tuesday through Thursday – 9:30 am to 5:15 pm; Friday and Saturday – 9:30 am to 8:45 pm; Sunday – 9:30 am to 5:15 pm; closed Monday.
It is imperative that you stop at the front information desk because of the enormous size. Decide what one or two exhibitions you want to see and get directions. In spring, fall or summer, be sure to include the roof Sculpture Garden Café. The view of Central Park is unreal! My other favorite is the Temple of Dendur (a complete Egyptian temple enclosed in its own glass-domed wing). The Met also has wonderful concerts so check the schedule.

GUGGENHEIM MUSEUM, 1071 Fifth Avenue at 89th Street, 212-423-3500. Hours: Sunday through Wednesday – 10 am to 6 pm; Friday and Saturday – 10 am to 8 pm; closed Thursday.
Frank Lloyd Wright designed the museum, which has been controversial since it

opened in the late '50s. You walk up a spiral ramp viewing changing exhibits of modern art. The permanent collection of impressionist to contemporary art is housed on the side galleries of the second level.

FRICK COLLECTION, 1 East 70th Street at Fifth Avenue, 212-288-0700. Hours: Tuesday through Saturday–10 am to 6 pm; Sunday – 1 pm to 6 pm; closed Monday. A former private residence filled with international masterpieces including those by Vermeer and Rembrandt. It is like walking through someone's elegant mansion. I have to resist sitting down and pretending that this is my house. The 18th century furniture collection is as superb as the old masters' paintings and sculptures.

THE ASIA SOCIETY, 725 Park Avenue at East 70th Street, 212-288-6400. Hours: Tuesday through Saturday – 11 am to 6 pm; Thursday – 11am to 8 pm; Sunday – Noon to 5 pm; closed Monday. Permanent Asian Art Collection of John D. Rockefeller, III plus fascinating changing exhibits. Don't miss the lovely terrace on the second floor – a great spot for a quiet moment.

GUGGENHEIM MUSEUM–SOHO, 575 Broadway at Prince near Houston, 212-423-3500. Hours: Sunday, Monday, Thursday, Friday and Saturday – 11 am to 6 pm; closed Tuesday and Wednesday. Exhibits of contemporary art as well as changing exhibits from the permanent Guggenheim collection. The ambiance of this renovated SoHo loft building is one of terrific space without hordes of people.

THE CLOISTERS, Fort Tryon Park at 191st Street, 212-923-3700. Hours: Tuesday through Sunday – 9:30 am to 5:15 pm; closed Monday. Medieval art and architecture collection from the Metropolitan Museum of Art. Located at the north end of Manhattan with gorgeous views of the Hudson River. Here you can take a subway or a $15 to $20 taxi ride but it is like visiting a medieval cloister in Europe; a special beautiful place.

LOWER EAST SIDE TENEMENT MUSEUM, 90 Orchard Street at Broome Street, 212-431-0233. Hours: Tuesday, Wednesday, Friday–Noon to 5 pm; Thursday–Noon to 9 pm; Saturday and Sunday–11 am to 5 pm. Tours of three different immigrant apartments in a 19th century tenement building.

JEWISH MUSEUM, 1109 Fifth Avenue at 92nd Street, 212-423-3200. Hours: Sunday, Monday, Wednesday, Thursday– 11 am to 5:45 pm; Tuesday– 11 am to 8 pm; Closed Friday, Saturday and major Jewish holidays. Contains the largest U.S. collection of Judaica and special changing art collections. Housed in an elegant turn-of-the-century mansion built by the Warburg Family in 1908. The café on the lower level is a delightful spot for an inexpensive but delicious lunch. The museum has excellent exhibits of such Jewish painters as Pissaro, George Segal and Freund, to name a few.

MUSEUM OF AFRICAN ART, 593 Broadway between Houston and Prince Streets, 212-966-1313. Hours: Tuesday through Friday–10:30 am to 5:30 pm; Saturday and Sunday–Noon to 6 pm; closed Monday. The architect, Maya Lin, who designed the Washington D.C. Vietnam Veterans Memorial, renovated a 19th Century cast iron building into gallery space for a variety of African art. There are continuous changing exhibits from private African art collections and museums from around the world.

**THE STUDIO MUSEUM IN HARLEM,
144 West 125th Street, 212-864-4500.
Hours: Wednesday through Friday –
10 am to 5 pm; Saturday and Sunday –
1 pm to 6 pm.** A permanent collection of
African-American artists as well as changing exhibits in the heart of Harlem. I love
the small but stunning sculpture garden.
If you do not have a Hop-on Hop-off tour
bus ticket, I recommend calling a car service or taxi after your visit. It is often difficult to find a taxi on the street.

There are so many other outstanding
museums that space prevents me from
mentioning them all. Please consult the
NYC Guide for a complete list or *Artwise
Manhattan*, the museum map, and *Best
Museums — New York City* from Trip
Builder and the Sunday *New York Times*.

New York is a
shopper's paradise!

Shopping for Home, Family and Self

People come from all over the world to shop in New York. Just the number of stores of every variety will boggle your mind. They range from discount stores to outrageously overpriced but unique boutiques. Merchandise for your home, your pantry, your family and friends or yourself is waiting to tempt you into credit card overload. Be wary. Plan your shopping budget in advance and be strong — STICK TO IT! For detailed information, check the Resources List or *Born to Shop New York*, by Suzy Gershman. *Here are a few personal favorites by area:*

- **On Fifth Avenue between 55th and 59th Streets:** *Bergdorf Goodman* for terrific lingerie and international designer boutiques; *Henri Bendel* for elegant wearable fashions by Yeohlee, gifts and cosmetics; *Takashimaya* for lovely ambiance and beautiful home accessories.

- **On Madison Avenue between 50th and 90th Streets:** *Marolo* for affordable Italian shoes, *Eileen Fisher* for attractive comfortable fashions, *Frette* for gorgeous linens, *Shanghai Tang* for upscale Chinese and Western fashion and accessories and *Barney's* for the ultra chic.

- **On Broadway and Columbus from 65th to 90th Streets:** Great shopping for inexpensive china at *Fishs Eddy*, 77th and Broadway, also in *Chelsea* at 19th and Broadway.

- **Soho, South from Houston and West Broadway:** While browsing the galleries, watch for *Flower Shop* by David Browne, 399 Bleeker Street, *Zona* for household gift items, *Tehen* for "with it" French fashions, *Morgan Lefay* for floaty chiffon dresses (also on Madison Avenue) and *Kates Paperie* for handmade papers.

- **Little Italy, between Grand and Houston Streets and Prince and Mulberry Streets:** For cashmere — *Lucien Pellat Finet*, 226 Elizabeth Street; for moderately priced sportswear — *American Colors* by Henry Lehr, 232 Elizabeth Street; for soft feminine dresses for "Twiggy" bodies, *Tracy Feith*, 209 Mulberry street.

- **Chelsea, between 20th and 23rd Streets and Ninth and Tenth Avenues**: Among the wonderful galleries in this part of town are *Comme des Garcons*, a not-to-miss boutique with avant-garde expensive clothes tucked into an incredibly designed store at 520 West 22nd Street and *IS*, at 136 17th Street. This is a stunning stationery store designed by architect Robert Hirsch. The elegant paper products are the designs of Drew Souza. *IS* is closed Mondays.

- **Delancey and Orchard Streets:** *Feng Shiu,* 111 Eldridge Street, 212-219-1979, is an interesting Chinese contemporary art gallery with a Chinese American woman's art displayed at reasonable prices.

- **Chinatown, Mott and Canal Streets:** *Kam Man*, the Chinese supermarket, is one of my favorite places for small inexpensive holiday gifts. In the basement are beautiful packages of Chinese tea, covered teacups and stunning pottery from Japan at half the price of Uptown stores. On the main floor are sandalwood soaps at bargain prices. *Ten Ren Tea & Ginseng Company, Inc.,* 75 Mott Street, is an interesting store to buy rare exotic Chinese teas.

- **TriBeCa, Canal to Chambers street, Centre Street to West Side Highway:** Young hip warehouse-like stores for he, she and home. Do not miss the *A.B.C. Warehouse*.

- **Greenwich Village and East Village, West 14 Street to Houston Street, East River Drive to West Side Highway:** Interesting boutiques and antiques as well as vintage clothes and far-out punk. Fun for browsing.

DISCOUNT SHOPPING

- **CENTURY 21: 22 Cortland Street, near World Trade Center,** for off-price designer clothing plus housewares, shoes, accessories and menswear.

- **LOEHMANN'S: Ninth Avenue at 16th Street.** Located in the original Barney's, you never know what designer treasure you might find.

FLEA MARKETS AND ANTIQUES

- **SOHO ANTIQUES FAIR, 212-682-2000, Broadway and Grand Street.**

- **GREEN FLEA INDOOR/OUTDOOR MARKET:** Saturdays on the East Side at East 67th Street between First and York; Sundays on the West Side at Columbus and 77th Street. 212-721-0900.

Shopping for Gourmet and Ethnic Foods

Even if you are not a cook or a gourmet, do not miss visiting one of New York's fabulous food emporiums just for the experience. Because of the ethnic diversity of the population, it is possible to find special foods and herbs from almost anywhere on this planet. The overwhelming variety of food is tantalizing. I wish you luck in resisting; for me it is impossible. I feel compelled to have a little taste of this and that everywhere!

Wherever you walk, you will find your own favorites. (Send home non-perishables. Carry home smoked salmon, breads, pastas and cheeses.) *Here is a sampling:*

- **ZABARS: 2245 Broadway between 80th and 81st Streets, 212-787-2000.** One of the oldest West Side specialty food markets in New York. Buy a great picnic to enjoy in Central Park or a freshly baked croissant to munch on as you walk.

- **FAIRWAY MARKET:** 2127 Broadway between Seventh and Broadway, 212-595-1888. An incredible food emporium. You will think you have crossed the world's frontiers.

- **EATS BY ELI ZABAR:** 1064 Madison on Madison in the 80's, 212-772-2011. A smaller version of the original West Side Zabar's. Eli, a nephew, offers a magnificent array of foods and baskets of breads. The carryout counter is tantalizing and there is a café for lunch before visiting uptown museums.

- **THE VINEGAR FACTORY:** 431 East 91st Street, 212-987-0885. You might want to buy a few imported herbs and spices for hostess gifts or a prepared dinner to enjoy on your trip home. (Also owned by Eli Zabar.)

- **DEAN & DELUCCA:** Corner of Prince Street and Broadway in Soho, 212-226-6800. One of the original gourmet markets in New York with consistently high quality merchandise as well as steep prices. The coffee or tea choices are incredible.

- **BALDUCCIS:** 424 Sixth Avenue between 9th and 10th Streets in Greenwich Village, 212-673-2600. Just enjoy the aroma of this wonderful old market, one of the early gourmet food purveyors in New York.

- **SWEET CHEESE:** 141 Third Avenue between 14th and 15th Streets in Gramercy Park, 212-477-1221. A tiny stylish cheese boutique with homemade carryouts and fresh sandwiches.

Small Specialty
Food Stores and Bakeries

DOWNTOWN

- **BOULEY BAKERY:** (See page 39.) For incredible breads.

- **RAFFETOS:** 114 West Houston Street, 212-777-1261. Regulars have been lining up for years for hand-cut pasta specialties that melt in your mouth.

- **BALTHAZAR BAKERY:** 80 Spring Street, 212-965-1785. Offers an assortment of breads as well as carryout foods.

- **DI PALO DAIRY:** 206 Grand Street, 212-226-1033. Specializes in all kinds of delectable cheeses.

LITTLE ITALY,
CHINATOWN AND SOHO

Start walking on Grand and Mott in
Little Italy and cross Canal Street to the
heart of Chinatown — or sit down and
enjoy a latte with your Italian pastry or
biscotti in Little Italy before crossing into
Chinatown. In Chinatown, the sweet bean
cakes, cookies and pastries are really
sweet. It is fun to stop in at the dozens of
bakeries that line the streets and just point
to a pastry and enjoy it on your walk
through these fascinating neighborhoods.

LOWER EAST SIDE:
DELANCEY/ORCHARD STREET
NEIGHBORHOOD

*Many of the Jewish merchants close
their stores on Saturday.*

■ **THE SWEET LIFE: 63 Hester Street at
Ludlow Street, 212-598-0092, Sunday –
Friday, 9 am to 6 pm.** Gorgeous hand-
dipped chocolates, beautiful gift baskets
and trays, candies and dried fruit and
nuts from around the world.

- **KADORESI & SONS: 51 Hester Street, 212-677-5441.** Imported dried fruits, nuts, candies, spices, coffee and tea and many interesting Israeli products.

- **KASSAR'S BIALYS: 39 Essex Street, 212-387-9940.** Fresh baked bagels, bialys and challahs (Jewish egg breads).

- **RATNERS RESTAURANT & BAKERY: 138 Delancey Street, 212-677-5588.** A traditional Jewish restaurant and bakery — an old landmark.

CHELSEA

- **CHELSEA MARKET: 75 Ninth Avenue between 15th and 16th Streets, 212-243-6005.** A converted warehouse that is home to several interesting food emporiums. Try one of Amy's breads — they are worth the calories! The big surprise here is **FREE SATURDAY AFTERNOON TANGO DANCING** inside the 10th Street entrance hosted by Triangalo Tango Studio. Dancing is usually from 4 to 7 pm. Call Triangalo Studio to confirm the time, 212-633-6445.

HARLEM

- **MAKE MY CAKE:** 110th Street, corner of Lenox, 212- 932-0833, and 2380 Seventh Avenue, corner of 139th Street, 212-231-2344. Specialties include carrot cake, peach cobbler, sweet potato and apple pie and the latest invention, sweet potato cheese cake — pure heaven!

An overview...

See New York in three days.

How to See New York: A Sample Three-Day Overview

FRIDAY (DAY 1)

➢ **10–10:30 am:** Try for an early arrival. Check into your hotel and leave your bag with the bellman (tip $2). Rooms are generally not ready until noon or 1 pm. Walk to 58th and Fifth Avenue to Bergdorf Goodman (across from the Plaza Hotel).

➢ **10:30–11:15 am:** Shop Bergdorf's — check out your favorite designers, shoe departments or the fabulous lingerie.

➢ **11:15–Noon:** Turn right when leaving Bergdorf's and cross 57th Street passing posh shops to Henri Bendel on Fifth Avenue at 56th Street. First stop: the wearable, packable Yeohlee collection on the top floor. Next, the gift boutique and the main floor for chic costume jewelry and great cosmetics.

➢ **Noon–1:30 pm:** Cross Fifth Avenue at 55th Street and have lunch at the Japanese department store, Takashimaya in the Tea Box on the lower level. Visit

the flower shop on the main floor, and
then take the elevator up to three for
the beautiful home accessories from
around the world. This is one of the
most elegant stores in New York.

➤ **1:30–1:45 pm:** Continue down Fifth
Avenue to 53rd Street. Watch for St.
Thomas Church. Cross Fifth Avenue
and turn right for one-half block to
the Museum of Modern Art (MoMA)
entrance.

➤ **1:45–3 pm:** Wander through this world-
class museum, enjoying the collection
of 19th and 20th century art. If the
weather is good, linger for a few minutes in the sculpture garden.

➤ **3–3:45 pm:** Exit museum and turn
left, back to Fifth Avenue. Turn right at
the corner (53th Street) and walk four
blocks to Rockefeller Center. Enjoy the
terraced gardens, then continue past
them to view the outdoor summer terrace, which becomes the skating rink in
winter. In the building on the opposite
side of the terrace, take the elevator
up to the 65th floor to the bar of the
Rainbow Room. Enjoy a glass of wine
while you take in the incredible view.

Now, it is your choice. Return to your hotel, unpack and rest or...

➤ **3:45–5 pm:** Cross Fifth Avenue. Check out the windows at Saks Fifth Avenue. Cross 49th Street and peek into St. Patrick's Cathedral. Take a taxi to 72nd and Madison Avenue. Wander Madison Avenue back to 60th Street—window shopping all of the famous European and American designer boutiques like Armani, Krizia, Valentino, St. Laurent, DNKY, Calvin Klein, Ralph Lauren and Eileen Fisher to name a few. You will also find dozens of art, antique and gift galleries.

➤ **5–5:30 pm:** Turn left at 60th Street— walk two blocks to Lexington Avenue. Turn right and voila you are at Bloomingdale's. Run in for a quick look. I recommend shopping the perfume or cosmetics counters for a few small gifts. If you are really into shopping, return on Saturday for an extended visit.

➤ **5:30–5:45 pm:** Turn right on 57th Street passing more famous stores such as Channel, Hermes and Tourneau Watches, and look up to the second floor windows of a few important art galleries like Pace and Wildenstein. Return to your hotel.

➢ **5:45–6:30 pm:** Unpack and freshen up for your evening at the theater.

➢ **6:45–7:45 pm:** Enjoy your pre-theater supper (perhaps at Orso, Tout Va Bien, LaCrepe de Bretagne or Trattoria dell'Arte). Save dessert for after theater when you are not so rushed.

➢ **7:45–8 pm:** Walk or take a taxi to your theater.

➢ **8–10:15/11 pm:** After theater—if you see a taxi, grab it and take the taxi back to your hotel. Choose a nearby restaurant, coffee shop or hotel bar for dessert or a drink. However if there are huge crowds and no taxi, find a place (there are dozens of restaurants and bars in the theater district) and have your drink or dessert there. It will be easier later to find a taxi home.

➢ **Midnight:** Crawl into your bed and enjoy a well-earned rest!

SATURDAY (DAY 2)

➢ **9:30–10:45 am:** Take a taxi (about $12) to Battery Park for the Staten Island Ferry. The trip costs 50 cents and you will get a quick look at Ellis Island and the Statue of Liberty as well as a terrific view of Manhattan from the water.

➢ **10:45–11:30 am:** Walk the boardwalk at Battery Park over to Robert Wagner Park where the new Museum of Jewish Heritage is located. In the park is a tall brown post and lintel structure like a large door frame; look through the frame to the river and you will see the best "framed" view of the Statue of Liberty. Don't laugh but the structure actually houses the public restrooms! Only in New York! Next, stand in the park looking past the gardens at the Hudson River and Manhattan. What a view! Be sure not to miss the wonderful Jim Dine sculpture in the garden.

➢ **11:30 am:** Take a taxi to the Lower East Side Tenement Museum, 90 Orchard Street at Broome Street. Here you can see three different families' apartments from 1860–1930. You will feel as though they were your relatives. Tours start on the hour and last one hour. There is no admission without the tour. I recommend calling 212-431-0233 ahead to

reserve your space on the noon tour.
(While waiting for the noon tour, watch
the film in the side room.) Remember,
since this is Saturday, many of the local
Jewish shops are closed.

➣ **1–1:50 pm:** Leaving the museum,
turn left on Delancey Street. Walk a few
blocks to Elizabeth Street. Turn right and
you will see the new boutiques in Little
Italy. Continue to Houston Street — find
a taxi and go to Mrs. Mendl's Tea Room
in the Inn at 56 Irving Place where you
have reserved a 2 pm tea. 212-533-4466.

➣ **2–3:30 pm:** Enjoy your tea!! (Smoked
salmon sandwiches, scones with clotted
crème, cookies, fruit and chocolate covered strawberries.)

➣ **3:45–4:15 pm:** Leave Mrs. Mendl's —
turn left on Irving Place and turn right
on 17th Street walking through Gramercy
Park to Chelsea. Stop in the beautiful
stationery store IS (136–17th Street)
and buy a few pieces of elegant paper.

> **4:15–5 pm:** Watch or participate in the tango dancing at the Chelsea Market. (See page 72.) If you want to dance, there are always single men who will approach you. Unfortunately there is no air-conditioning in the summer so you might prefer watching. This is really a New York happening!

> **5 pm:** Walk Uptown on Ninth Avenue to the Chelsea art galleries between Ninth and Tenth Avenues and 20th to 23rd Street. Stop for a refreshing drink at Tea Lily on 22nd Street before taking a taxi back to your hotel.

> **6:30–7:30 pm:** Rest and dress before the evening performance at Lincoln Center. Since you had a late tea you won't need supper until after the performance.

➤ **7:30 pm:** Take a taxi to Lincoln Center or walk "if you still have feet."

➤ **8–10:45 pm:** Attend the performance, enjoying a sandwich at one of the bars during intermission. They are under $5 and perfect for a snack to sustain you before dinner. If you are at the Metropolitan Opera House, you can order a dessert for intermission in the dining room on the Grand Tier level.

➤ **10:45 pm:** The choice is yours. Stop for an appetizer, dinner or dessert. Splurge, moderate or inexpensive. Just be sure that you reserve ahead of time.

➤ **Midnight:** Sweet dreams!

SUNDAY (DAY 3)

➤ **10 am–12:30 pm:** Check out of your
hotel and leave your bag with the bellman — again give him a few dollars.
Walk through Central Park to the
Metropolitan Museum (choose one or
two galleries to visit) or take a two-hour
guided bicycle tour through Central
Park (it is $30 — reserve at 212-541-8759)
or a horse and buggy ($65) for an hour.

➤ **12:45–1:30 pm:** Visit the Frick
Collection.

➤ **1:30–2:45 pm:** Cut through Central Park
to the West Side and have brunch at the
Café des Artistes, Café Luxembourg
or one of the little cafés that dot
Broadway or Amsterdam Avenue. If
you just want a sandwich or an omelet,
try Maximillian on Seventh Avenue.

➤ **2:45–3:45 pm:** Visit upper West Side shops and food stores like *Zabars* and *Fairway Market*. For great discounted dishes, overruns and hotel china, stop at *Fishs Eddy* on 77th Street and Broadway. (Also, stop to watch the wall climbers on Broadway at 63rd Street scale a five-foot wall.)

➤ **4 pm:** Return to your hotel, pick up your bag and take a taxi or prearranged van or car service to the airport for your late afternoon flight (preferably 6 to 7 pm).

Au revoir New York!
(Hopefully you can sleep on the plane!)

A Few Suggestions for Next-Timers, Many-Timers or Fourth-Day Visitors

➢ **Chinatown and Little Italy ($1\frac{1}{2}$ – $2\frac{1}{2}$ hours):** Have lunch in a noodle shop. Shop the basement of *Kam Man Market* and *Ten Ren Tea & Ginseng Company*, crossing over to Little Italy for biscotti and latte.

➢ **Ellis Island ($2\frac{1}{2}$ – $3\frac{1}{2}$ hours):** Take the ferry and visit this historical American sight which today is a wonderful museum. When you return, visit the new Museum of Jewish Culture in the park.

➢ **Take a Walking Tour (2 hours):** Free from *Big Apple Greeter* — any neighborhood you'd like to visit. (I loved my recent tour of Greenwich Village with Sybil White, a very personable and knowledgeable guide.) Call 212-669-8270.

➢ **Visit Harlem (2–3 hours):** Visit either
on your own or with a tour. See *NYC Guide*
for tour possibilities or ask *Big Apple
Greeter* for a volunteer guide. They need a
week to ten days notice. Sample visit:

> Lunch at *Londels* – then walk east
> on 139th Street to see the beautiful
> *Striver's Row Historic Townhouses.*
> Stop at the corner of 139th and
> Seventh Avenue at *Make My Cake*
> for the sweet potato pie cheesecake.
> Just don't count calories. Next visit
> the *Abyssinian Baptist Church* before
> going over to the *Studio Museum* or
> *Schomburg Center.*

➢ **Lower East Side (1½ hours):** Walk
down Hester Street with its exotic
diverse food, candy, spice and bakery
shops. Stop at *Feng Shiu* (the Chinese
American artist-owned gallery) where
you'll discover lovely feminine contemporary Chinese art. Visit the historic
Eldridge Street Synagogue, one of New
York's earliest houses of worship and
social centers. The entire neighborhood
is a veritable United Nations with Jews,
Italians, Spaniards, Vietnamese, Chinese,
African-Americans, etc., etc., all living
and working side by side.

➢ **A United Nations tour and lunch
(2 – 2 ½ hours):** Reserve for lunch
Monday – Friday in the *Delegates Dining
Room.* The chef prepares cuisine from
around the world. The setting over the
East River, the exotic foods and the international diners (many in native dress)
make this a memorable experience.
Security is tight so you will be checked
in. 212-963-7626 **OR** just take a tour and
dine at Marichu on East 46th Street
(1 – 1 ½ hours).

➢ **A real pick-me-up (1–2 hours):** A
manicure at the Salon at the *Wyndham
Hotel* (42 West 58th Street, 212-753-6131).
A facial or makeup at *Allure,* 139 E. 55th
Street, 212-644-5500. Then shop *Felissimo,*
10 West 56th Street, for beautiful home
accessories or visit a small but wonderful
museum like *Abigail Adams Smith,
Dahesh Museum, Museum of American
Crafts or St. Patrick's Cathedral* on
Fifth Avenue.

➢ **Shop Upper East Side boutiques,
galleries and food emporiums (2–3
hours):** Visit the *Whitney Museum,
Asia House,* and the *Cooper Hewett
National Design Museum* with its won-
derful garden or the *Jewish Museum.*
The *Conservancy Gardens* in Central
Park at 105th Street and the *Museo del
Barrio* are other choices.

➢ **Take a taxi to the extraordinary medieval museum the** *Cloisters* **(2½ – 3 hours.):** The view overlooking the Hudson is amazing.

➢ **SoHo (2½ – 3½ hours):** Have lunch and visit the galleries, boutiques and cafés.

➢ **Three New York City jewels (2½ – 3½ hours):** *Grand Central Station, Pierpont Morgan Library* and the *New York Public Library* at 42nd and Fifth, followed by a lovely lunch in *Bryant Park* at the *Grill* or *Café.*

➢ **Take an art tour of New York (2 hours):** *Art Horizons,* 212-969-9410, or a boat tour with lunch (2 ½ hours), *Bateau* 212-352-2022.

These are just a few

of my favorite places!

After three days, you will have

your own favorite places.

Before starting

your New York odyssey,

be sure to have the essentials

New York Essentials

ARRIVAL-NEW YORK-MORNING

Arriving by Plane – Remember there are three major airports: LaGuardia and Kennedy in New York and Newark in New Jersey.

- Try to arrive at LaGuardia. It is closest to the City and has the least expensive cab fare and fastest route into the City (about 30 minutes).

Transportation Choices:

- Bus from Kennedy, LaGuardia or Newark to bus station in Manhattan for about $10 or dial *Blue Van* 1-800-258-3826. (Takes eight passengers to their hotel for about $15-$16.) Your travel agent or hotel also can arrange a car service.

- If taking a bus, take a taxi to your hotel from the bus station. A Midtown taxi is under $5.

- Taxi from LaGuardia to Midtown with the bridge tolls and tip is under $25 and Kennedy to Midtown is about $30.

However, a taxi from Newark is more than $45 so it is the bus or *Blue Van* for most folks. Taxi tip is 15 percent.

Arrival Hotel:

- Tip the doorman $1 and register at the desk.

- Tip the bellman $2 for showing you to your room. Before he leaves, make sure the lights and television work and that there are fresh wash cloths and towels.

- Note where the emergency exits are from your room.

- If you like quiet, request a back room on the courtyard, instead of one on the street.

- Remember, Fifth Avenue divides New York into East and West Side.

- Use Automated Teller Machines (ATM) only in the daytime, preferably inside a bank or crowded building — $100 in cash is usually more than enough. Traveler's checks and credit cards are safer.

Before starting your New York odyssey, be sure to have with you:

- Hotel card or brochure in your purse, along with a small city map.

- Ten dollars in singles for tips, taxis and nibbles, preferably in a pocket so that you do not have to open your purse.

- A credit card (Visa, MasterCard or American Express) with an available credit limit of $1,000 to cover emergencies.

- A telephone calling card.

Tipping Guidelines:

- **Maids:** $3 to $5 a night depending on service and how fancy the hotel. Leave the tip on the bureau.

- **Hotel concierges or exceptional front desk clerk:** $5 to $10 per day.

- **Restaurants:** 15 percent to 20 percent in a moderate to expensive restaurant, depending on the service.

Other Essential Guidelines:

- **Dining:** Call or ask hotel staff to reserve a table for dining. Select a restaurant close to your hotel or evening's entertainment to save on cab fare.

- **Tickets:** Decide if you want to take a chance on half-price tickets for performances or "must see" a specific event. Book full-price tickets ahead from home, charging them to your credit card. It is still cheaper than paying a

scalper's surcharge. If it is a last minute
trip and you are willing to pay, the hotel
can usually find tickets or you can stand
in line at TKTS Booth, 47th Street and
Broadway, for 25 percent discounted
tickets — 50 percent off plus $2.50 sur-
charge on day of performance. They
take ONLY CASH. 212-768-1818.

- **Purchases:** If you send your purchases
  home you won't need to carry them.
  When items are sent out of state, you
  will save the New York sales tax. United
  Parcel Service (UPS) is reasonable, and
  opening packages after you return home
  extends the fun of the trip. For example,
  In New York, the 8 percent sales tax on
  a $300 purchase is $24. Depending on the
  weight, UPS is approximately $5 to $6.

- **Checkout:** Most hotels require you to
  vacate your room before noon. Leave
  your baggage with the bellman. Tip him
  $2 at this point and another $2 when you
  pick up your baggage. Inquire at the front
  desk about the time you should depart
  for the airport and decide on your means
  of transportation (taxi, bus, car service or
  van). If you want a car service, book
  ahead. I use *Tel Aviv* 212-777-7777. To
  Newark with tip and tolls is about $45.
  They take credit cards.

- Plan to arrive at the airport one hour before the flight. Call before leaving to make sure your flight has not been delayed or canceled.

- Make sure you have reading material with you. It will help pass the time, especially if there are delays.

- If you are checking your bag and it isn't a bright color, attach a few brightly colored ribbons to help you spot it quickly at baggage claim.

- Tip the porter $2 per bag.

- Arrange airport transportation before your trip. If you are not driving yourself, ask a friend for a ride or call a car service. Give the person picking you up your flight schedule so he or she can call and check on the time of arrival and decide on the meeting location.

By now you should be

thoroughly energized and ready

to plan your next adventure.

Watch for the next *Going like Lynn!*

RESOURCE LISTS AND IMPORTANT PHONE NUMBERS

❶ New York City Visitors &
Convention Bureau: 212-484-1200
or 1-800 NYCVISIT (New York
City Visitors Counselors):
212-484-1222. 810 Seventh
Avenue, New York 10018.

❷ Sunday *New York Times*.

❸ Listings and Reviews – *New Yorker*
and *New York Magazine*.

❹ Your local library or bookstore
travel book section.

A few favorites:

- *Best Museums NY City*
  from *Trip Builder*.

- *Hidden Treasures NY City*
  from *Trip Builder*.

- *Artwise Manhattan*
  (The Museum Map).

- *New York for the Independent
  Traveler* (wonderful step-by-step
  itineraries for walking tours) by
  Ruth Humleker.

97

RESOURCE LISTS AND IMPORTANT PHONE NUMBERS

- *Born to Shop New York,* by Suzy Gershman.

- *Hippocrene USA Guide to Black New York.*

- Green *Michelin Guide for New York* and whatever other books catch your fancy.

❺ A necessity: *Zagat Survey New York City Restaurants.* This is the most comprehensive New York restaurant guide. It offers good information and reliable ratings.

❻ A few small delightful publications that I found at a small press book fair:

- *Best Bistros and Brasseries* by Robert P. Seass, 212-255-4616 or email: bistrobob@aol.com.

- *Good and Cheap Ethnic Eats in New York City* by Robert Sietsema, published by City & Company, 22 West 23rd Street, New York 10010, 212-366-1988.

- *New York Book of Tea* by Bo Niles and Veronica McNiff, also published by City & Company.

RESOURCE LISTS AND IMPORTANT PHONE NUMBERS

❼ Hotel concierge

❽ Current *NYC Guide* and *Where Magazine* (free in hotel).

❾ Tours:

- *Big Apple Greeter,* 212-669-8270.

- *New York Apple Tours Hop-on Hop-Off* 2-Day Bus Tickets, 212-944-9200 or 800-876-9868.

- *Art Horizons,* 212-969-9410.

- *Central Park Bicycle Tours,* 212-541-8759.

- Boat Tours:

  Bateaux New York, 212-352-2022.

  Circle Line, 212-563-3200.

❿ Horse and Buggy Rides, on 59th Street from Fifth to Eighth Avenue ($35 first half-hour, $15 each additional quarter-hour).

RESOURCE LISTS AND IMPORTANT PHONE NUMBERS

⑪ TKTS Booth, 47th and Broadway and at the World Trade Center, 25 percent to 50 percent off tickets for Broadway or Off Broadway shows plus a small fee. Tickets for day of performance CASH ONLY 212-768-1818. Lines are shorter at the TKTS booth at the World Trade Center. Or get half-price tickets on-line at www.playbill.com. You can order in advance and it beats standing in line.

⑫ **Car Service** (or ask your travel agent or hotel concierges):

- *Tel Aviv,* 212-777-7777.

- *Sabra,* 212-777-7171.

⑬ **A few Beauty Breaks:**

- *All of the department stores offer full beauty services.*

- Long time favorite: *Elizabeth Arden,* Fifth Avenue at 57th Street, 212-546-0200.

RESOURCE LISTS AND IMPORTANT PHONE NUMBERS

- Very today: *Henri Bendel,* Fifth Avenue between 56th and 57th Streets, *212-247-1100.*

- A complete spa: *Allure,* 139 East 55th Street, 212-644-5500.

- Very friendly: *The Salon at the Wyndham,* 42 West 58th Street, 212-753-6131.

Additional Resources: For a complete list, contact *NYC Visitors & Convention Bureau Guide Book.*

Going like Lynn©

A Series of Liberating
Travel Primers for Women

For information about a
personal travel consultation,
call Lynn Portnoy toll free at

1-888-386-9688

Or visit lynn on the internet:

goinglikelynn.com

*For book orders, please use the
order form on the following page.*

Going like Lynn

A Series of Liberating Travel Primers for Women

Order Form

Quantity

Going like Lynn–Paris
$12.95 plus $2.75 shipping & handling
($15.70 total). *Add $1.10 shipping &
handling for each additional copy.*

Going like Lynn–New York
$13.95 plus $2.75 shipping & handling
($16.70 total). *Add $1.10 shipping &
handling for each additional copy.*

*Special Purchase: Going like
Lynn–Paris and New York Set*
$24 plus $2.75 shipping & handling
($26.75 total). *Add $1.50 shipping &
handling for each additional set.*

*Make checks payable to: Diamond Publishers.
Include check with order form and mail to:*

Diamond Publishers
29260 Franklin Rd, Suite 123
Southfield, Michigan 48034

To order by phone call 1-888-386-9688

Please print when completing form below:

☐ VISA   ☐ MasterCard

Name ....

Address ....

City................................... State............ Zip..............

Telephone ....

Card # ....

Expiration Date ....

Amount to be charged: ....

Signature ....